In the name of Allah,
the Most Beneficent, the Most Merciful

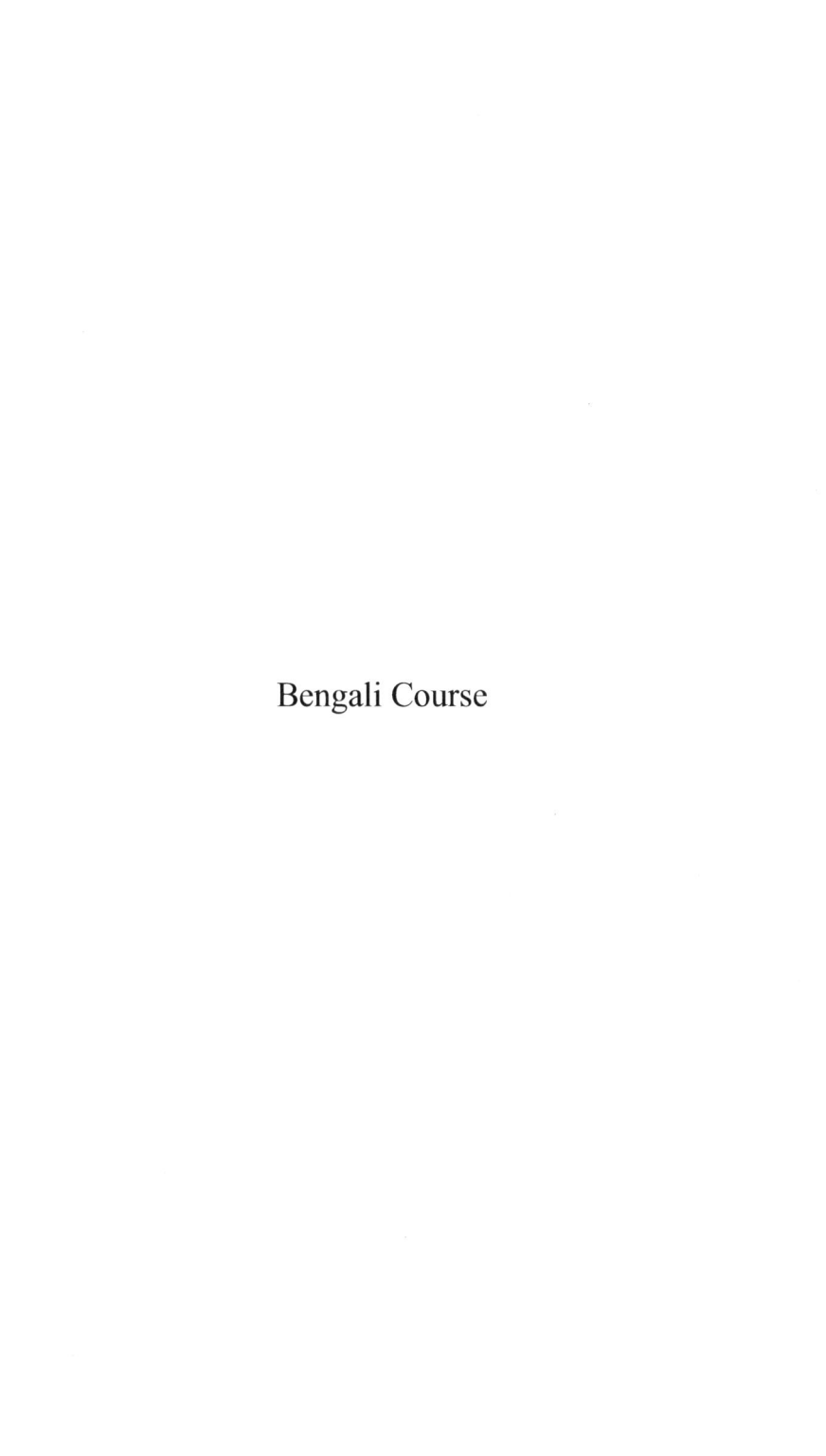

Bengali Course

Bengali Course
FOR ENGLISH-SPEAKING STUDENTS

BEGINNER TO INTERMEDIATE
Learn it. Speak it. Read it.

Aleur Rahman

Dedicated to mum and dad.
To whom without which nothing is possible.

…and to my nephews and nieces. The next generation of Bangladeshis. Stay young. Stay smart. Stay fresh.

About the author

Born but not bred, Bangladesh has always been my home. Whilst England has been, for the most part, my country of residence. Although I did not have the opportunity to spend my early years in Bangladesh, the Bengali language has always been integral to the way in which we would communicate at home.

Unfortunately, it was only the spoken language we had employed, whilst the written and grammatical appreciation of the language was overlooked. We lived in a time where the internet and technology were on the rise. Learning mainstream subjects in school and keeping up with the modern world around us became a priority. Ultimately the Bengali language was overlooked. This stoic mindset was to my own detriment as I found much later and after a belated visit to Bangladesh, that without knowledge of one's own mother tongue, one is but an empty shell of a man. Foreign to his own heritage and culture. A guest in his own home.

Thus while I have since attained a firm grasp of the Bengali language, I wish to pass this knowledge on to my fellow nationals.

Today, I am a structural engineer by profession, entrepreneur by compulsion, indie author by interest, a baker by nature, and "tea-maker" by obligation! And while that all sounds great, I am most proud of my Bangladeshi heritage by origin.

A brief history of the Bengali Language

Bengali, known by its endonym Bangla, is the national language in the People's Republic of Bangladesh. It is also the official language of West Bengal, Tripura, Assam and a few Islands in the territory of India.

In tandem with other Eastern Indo-Aryan languages, Bengali evolved approximately between the 10th and 12th century from Sanskrit and Magadhi Prakrit. The modern literary form of Bengali, however, was developed during the late 19th and early 20th centuries. Thus relatively recently. Of course, with Bangladesh gaining independence in 1971, this is not entirely a surprise.

When the Dominium of Pakistan was formed by the partition of India in 1947, Pakistan was composed of both West Pakistan and East Bengal (renamed East Pakistan in 1956). In 1948, the Government of Pakistan ordained Urdu as the sole national language, sparking much controversy as the majority (56 percent) of East Bengal (present-day Bangladesh) spoke Bengali. Thus sparking the Bengali Language Movement. A protest was organised on 21 February 1952 by students of the University of Dhaka (Dil and Dil 2011). When police killed 5 student and political activists, it provoked widespread civil unrest and public outrage. After years of unrest, the central government of Pakistan granted the official status of the Bengali Language in 1956. Thus the day of the protest and the following sacrifice was to be commemorated by the Language Movement Day, a national holiday in Bangladesh. Thus marking the Bengali Language the only language in the world to be also known for its language movement and its people sacrificing their life for their mother tongue. The

Shaheed Minar is a national monument in Dhaka, Bangladesh, established to commemorate this.

Today the Bengali language is the sixth most spoken language in the world. The second most spoken language in India. It is the language in which both the national anthems of Bangladesh and India were initially written.

Table of Contents

Introduction ix
Getting Started... xii

Lesson 1.0 – The Bengali Alphabet...1
Lesson 2.0 – a Diacritic form of the vowels.............................8
Lesson 3.0 – Forming words. Nouns 18
Lesson 4.0 – Adjectives 25
Lesson 5.0 – Adjective. Colour 30
Lesson 6.0 – a Possessive form of nouns............................. 37
Lesson 7.0 – Numbers. 1-10.. 44
Lesson 8.0 – Pronouns 53
Lesson 9.0 – Possessive Pronouns... 59
Lesson 10.0 – Forming words. Proper Nouns..................... 67
Lesson 11.0 – Numbers. 1-100 84
Lesson 12.0 – Forming words. Plural Nouns 101

All new words.. 106
Additional words.. 113
Bibliography.. 117

Introduction

Do you find yourself unable to read and speak Bengali? Constantly trying to keep up with conversations? Overwhelmed by the aunties and uncles on Eid? Stuttering with particular words knowing full well you do not have a speech defect? Mixing English with Bengali to complete a sentence? "Eye-balling" the room, hoping no one catches you out? Need help overcoming such situations? Clueless about where to begin?

This book will take you through the basics of the Bengali language, to a point where you no longer feel overwhelmed by Bengali conversation. The first chapter "Getting started" introduces two principal methods of learning. Applying these to the subsequent chapters will allow you to learn how to put Bengali letters together to form words and ultimately how these words form sentences used in everyday conversation. Master the use of nouns, adjectives and the possessive form of nouns thereafter. The first six lessons alone will elevate your knowledge of Bengali above par. Sufficient to impress your family members and friends. With the introduction of numbers and pronouns in the later chapters, you will be able to further utilise the language in a range of situations and settings.

The principal pages of this book accumulate to just over a hundred pages. A total of twelve chapters. Each chapter is precise and efficient. The reader is introduced solely to the information and principles required, with an example clause to ensure a firm understanding of the grammatical techniques and patterns introduced. Each chapter is then concluded with a collation of the new words, which are further utilised in the corresponding chapters. While the book may not be expansive in its coverage, it provides a firm grounding of the basic knowledge to which the reader can further build on.

The intention of this book, therefore, is to assume in its entirety that the reader has no access to video tutorials, audio guidance or a personal tutor. The book will solely take an individual from a non-Bengali speaking (and reading) status to a reasonably comfortable, Bengali-speaking individual who is able to read Bengali text on the move. On billboards, product labels and even newspapers. With the precise use of phonetics and English word comparisons (partial transliterations), one is able to sit comfortably, whether at home, abroad or on a plane and master the Bengali language. The sixth most spoken language in the world.

Read, learn and most importantly, enjoy. For without love and passion for what we do, why do we do what we do?!

Getting started

Before embarking on this journey, the reader is introduced to two principle methods of learning. Both methods ensure efficient and precise learning.

(a) Pronouncing letters

Due to the nature of learning a new language, each letter and syllable of a word will be expressed in a phonetic sound (phoneme) and compared to a similar English word (partial transliteration) to further compliment the correct pronunciation.

Letter example:

Bengali Letter	ব
Phoneme	"BO"
Partial transliteration (only pronounce the letters underlined & bold)	**Bo**ard *

*pronounce the full word. Than bold and underlined letters only

Word example:

Bengali word	বই
Phonemes	"BO" + "E"
Partial transliteration (only pronounce the letters underlined & bold)	**Bo**ard + **Ea**gle
Transliteration	boi
Translation	Book

Hence the sounds of each Bengali letter (unknown to the reader) can be precisely attained by extracting sounds from

English words (known to the reader). Thus avoiding the need for audio guidance.

(b) Pronouncing declined letters

When Bengali letters are put together to form a word, sometimes the major sound of the last letter is used to dominate while the remainder is left silent.

Letter example:

Bengali Letter	ল
Phoneme	"LO"
Partial transliteration (only pronounce the letters underlined & bold)	**Lo**rry *

*pronounce the full word. Than bold and underlined letters only**

Word example:

Bengali word	বল
Phonemes	"BO" + "∣L∣"
Partial transliteration (only pronounce the letters underlined & bold)	**Bo**ard + **L**orry
Transliteration	bol
Translation	Ball

Thus you will note where the phoneme of a Bengali letter is placed between two vertical lines, this dominates and the remaining sound becomes silent. Rather than expressing ল as "LO", we only touch the first part of the syllable with our tongue, ∣L∣.

Lesson 1.0 - The Bengali Alphabet

Vowels

Table 1.1 – Vowels (also referred to as graphemes as they are the smallest unit in the Bengali writing system)

অ	আ	ই	ঈ
"O"	"AH"	ROSHO-"E"	DIRGO-"E"
<u>o</u>r	<u>a</u>pple	<u>ea</u>gle	<u>ea</u>gle
উ	ঊ	ঋ	৯
ROSHO-"OO"	DIRG"OW"	"RI"	"LI"
<u>Oo</u>ps!	<u>Oo</u>ps!	<u>re</u>ad	<u>le</u>an
এ	ঐ	ও	ঔ
"AE"	"OI"	"OU"	"OW"
p<u>ay</u>	<u>oi</u>ntment	<u>o</u>r	t<u>oe</u>

*reader will note the apparent repetition of certain phonemes. Although some pairs sound similar, the second of the two is usually more emphasized. Thus its use depends on a particular word.

Consonants

Table 1.2 – Consonants

ক	খ	গ	ঘ	ঙ
"KO"	"KHO"	"GO"	"GHO"	UMO
college	**co**llege	**go**ne	**go**ne	eati**ng**
চ	ছ	জ	ঝ	ঞ
"CHO"	"CHHO"	Borgeo-"JO"	"JHO"	"NEO"
chop	**cho**p	**jaw**	**jaw**	**Leo**
ট	ঠ	ড	ঢ	ণ
"TOW"	"TTOW"	"DOW"	"DDHOW"	Murdaino-"NO"
towed	**to**wed	**door**	**door**	**no**rmal
ত	থ	দ	ধ	ন
"THOW"	"TTHOW"	"DHOW"	"DDHOW"	Dantio-"NO"
taught	**tau**ght	**dho**ti	**dho**ti	**no**rmal
প	ফ	ব	ভ	ম
"POW"	"FOW"	"BO"	"BHOW"	"MO"
to**po**logy	**four**	**bo**ard	**bo**ard	**mo**re

য	র	ল	শ
Ontaistho-"JO"	RO	"LO"	"Thalobbyo-"SHO"
jockey	**ro**ar	**lo**rry	**sho**p

ষ	স	হ	ড়	ঢ়
Murdaino-"SHO"	Dantio-"SHO"	"HO"	Doy shando-"ROW"	Doy shando-"RHOW"
shop	**sho**p	**ho**p	**raw**	**raw**
য়	ৎ	০ং	০ঃ	ঁ
Ontaistho-"O"	Kondo-"THO"	Onushwar	Bishorgo	Chondro-bindu
or	**tho**ught	eati**ng**	*silent*	*silent*

Example 1.0

Forming words. Simple nouns by placing letters together.

First Consonant	Second Consonant	Bangla word	Partial transliteration
ব	ল	বল	**bo**ard + **l**orry

(bol) – Ball

First Consonant	Second Consonant	Bangla word	Partial transliteration
আ	ম	আম	**a**pple + **m**ore

(am) – Mango

First Consonant	Second Consonant	Bangla word	Partial transliteration
ই	ট	ইট	<u>ea</u>gle + <u>t</u>owed

(eat) – Brick

First Consonant	Second Consonant	Bangla word	Partial transliteration
এ	ক	এক	<u>e</u>gg + <u>k</u>ick

(ehk) – One

First Consonant	Second Consonant	Bangla word	Partial transliteration
র	স	রস	**ro**ar + **sh**op

(rosh) – Juice of a fruit / sap

First Consonant	Second Consonant	Bangla word	Partial transliteration
দ	ই	দই	**dho**ti + **ea**gle

(dhoy) – curd

First Consonant	Second Consonant	Bangla word	Partial transliteration
ব	ই	বই	**bo**y + **ea**gle

(boi) – Book

First Consonant	Second Consonant	Third Consonant	Bangla word	Partial transliteration
ক	ল	ম	কলম	**co**llege + **lo**rry + **m**ore

(kolom) – Pen

New words
নতুন শব্দ

Bangla word	Translation	Transliteration
বল	Ball	*bol*
আম	Mango	*ahm*
ইট	Brick	*eat*
এক	One	*ehk*
রস	Juice of a fruit	*rosh*
দই	Curd	*dhoy*
বই	Book	*boi*
কলম	Pen	*kolom*

Lesson 2.0 – a Diacritic form of the vowels

Diacritic Form

The Bengali script has a total of 11 **vowel graphemes**. The smallest unit of the Bengali script. Introduced in table 1.1. Each vowel grapheme has a corresponding **diacritic form**, with the exception of অ.

Table 2.1 – Diacritic form

Vowel graphemes	Diacritic form	Phoneme
অ	*	"o"
আ	◌া	"ah"
ই	◌ি	"i"
ঈ	◌ী	"i"
উ	◌ু	"oo"
ঊ	◌ূ	"oo"
ঋ	◌ৃ	"ri"
এ	ে◌	"e"
ঐ	ৈ◌	"oi"
ও	ে◌া	"o"
ঔ	ে◌ৗ	"ow"

*default inherent vowel. This sound already exists in every consonant, introduced in table 1.2 (i.e. "Ko", "Jo", "Ro", "Lo", "Mo" etc).

Notes

অ – The most common and recognizable vowel, yet hidden away in plain sight. The sound of this vowel is inherent (invisible) in every consonant letter. Thus pre-applied to all the consonant letters. Note how they end with the sound |O| in table 1.2.

For this reason, the letter/grapheme অ does not require a diacritic form while the remaining graphemes do.

ই ঈ & উ ঊ – Both sets of graphemes (vowels) express the same sound, |i| and |oo|, respectively. The redundancy stems from the time when this script was used to write Sanskrit. The grapheme ই expresses a short pronunciation |i| and grapheme ঈ expresses a long pronounciation |i|. Thus the reader will hold the sound on the tip of their tongue for slightly longer. Similarly, the grapheme উ expresses a short pronounciation |oo| and grapheme ঊ expresses a long pronounciation |oo|.

ঋ – This grapheme does not, in essence, represent a vowel phoneme as the consonant-vowel unit, রি (ri) dominates the sound. Again, a remnant from the Sanskrit history for the Bengali script. The grapheme is however included in the catalogue of vowels as it is found amongst Bengali script.

৯ – Similar to the application of grapheme ঋ (ri), this grapheme is also dominated by the unit লি (li). Unlike ঋ however, this grapheme was discarded as its usage was extremely limited.

9

Diacritic Application

Now that we know the diacritic form of the individual vowel graphemes, we can apply these to all consonant letters to forge new sounds. The consonant letter is **primary**, while the vowel grapheme is **secondary**. Note how the vowel grapheme is not attached as an independent letter but in its diacritic form. Together they form a **unit**.

Table 2.2 – Diacritic application

Primary Consonant	Diacritic application (Unit)	Phoneme	Partial transliteration
ক	ক *	"ko"	**co**p
ক	কা	"kah"	**ca**tch
ক	কি	"ki"	**ki**ss
ক	কী	"kī"	**ki**ss
ক	কু	"koo"	**coo**l
ক	কূ	"koo"	**coo**l
ক	কৃ	"kri"	**cri**sp
ক	কে	"keh"	**ke**nt
ক	কৈ	"koi"	de**coy**
ক	কো	"ko"	**coo**p
ক	কৌ	"kow"	co**coa**

* No need for an additional notation. অ (from table 2.1) is already and naturally applied to the consonant. Thus remains the same.

Example 2.0
Forming words with vowel notations

Diacritic application to consonant, ক only

Primary Consonant	Diacritic application (Unit)	Unit application (word)	Partial transliteration
ক	ক	কলা	<u>co</u>p + <u>la</u>mp

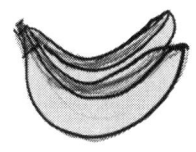

(ko-la) – Banana

Primary Consonant	Diacritic application (Unit)	Unit application (word)	Partial transliteration
ক	কা	নৌকা	<u>no</u> + <u>ca</u>tch

(no-ka) – Boat

Primary Consonant	Diacritic application (**Unit**)	Unit application (**word**)	Partial transliteration
ক	কি	**কি**	<u>ki</u>ss

(ki) – What

Primary Consonant	Diacritic application (**Unit**)	Unit application (**word**)	Partial transliteration
ক	কু	**কুকু**র	<u>co</u>ol + <u>co</u>ol + <u>r</u>ope

(ko-kor) - Dog

Primary Consonant	Diacritic application (Unit)	Unit application (word)	Partial transliteration
ক	কে	কে	<u>ke</u>ntucky

(keh) – Who

Primary Consonant	Diacritic application (Unit)	Unit application (word)	Partial transliteration
ক	কো	কোট	<u>coo</u>p + <u>t</u>ell
ক	কো	কোথায়	<u>coo</u>p + <u>thai</u>

(koot) - Coat

Example 2.1
Forming words with vowel notations

Diacritic application to random consonants

Primary Consonant	Diacritic application (Unit)	Unit application (word)	Partial transliteration
ন	ন	নদী	**no**rmal + **de**al

(noh-dhi) – River

Primary Consonant	Diacritic application (Unit)	Unit application (word)	Partial transliteration
চ	চা	চা	**cha**mp
প	পা	পাখি	**pa**rk + **ki**ss

(pah-ki) – Bird

Primary Consonant	Diacritic application (Unit)	Unit application (word)	Partial transliteration
ত	তি	হাতি	<u>ha</u>nd + <u>thi</u>ng

(ha-thi) – Elephant

Primary Consonant	Diacritic application (Unit)	Unit application (word)	Partial transliteration
ফ	ফু	ফুল	<u>foo</u>d + <u>l</u>amp
প	পু	পুতুল	<u>Poo</u>l + <u>Tw</u>o + <u>L</u>amp

(fool) – Flower

Primary Consonant	Diacritic application (Unit)	Unit application (word)	Partial transliteration
ব	বে	**বেলুন**	<u>be</u>ll + **loo** + |<u>**n**</u>|

(beh-loon) – Balloon

Primary Consonant	Diacritic application (Unit)	Unit application (word)	Partial transliteration
ট	টো	**টমেটো**	<u>to</u>p + <u>me</u>n + <u>**two**</u>
ঘ	ঘো	**ঘোড়া**	<u>**goo**</u> + <u>**ra**</u>j

(toh-meh-too) - Tomato

New words
নতুন শব্দ

Bangla word	Translation	Transliteration
কলা	Banana	*kola*
নৌকা	Boat	*noka*
কি?	What?	*ki*
কুকুর	Dog	*kokor*
কে?	Who?	*keh*
কোট	Coat	*koot*
কোথায়	Where?	*ko-thia*
নদী	River	*noh-dhi*
চা	Tea	*cha*
পাখি	Bird	*pahki*
হাতি	Elephant	*hathi*
ফুল	Flower	*fool*
পুতুল	Doll	*pootool*
বেলুন	Balloon	*behloon*
টমেটো	Tomato	*tomehtoo*
ঘোড়া	Horse	*goora*

Lesson 3.0 – Forming words. Nouns

Once the vowels, their appropriate diacritics (notations) and the consonants are understood, we can now move onto forming words. Note letters with the distinctive horizontal line running along the top are used to form Bengali words. "matra" (মাত্রা). Let us begin with nouns.

Nouns are used to identify a class of people, places or things.

Bengali word	এটা
Phoneme/s	"AE" + "Tah"
Partial transliteration (underlined & Bold)	p**ay** + **ta**n
Transliteration	ay-ta
Translation	this / this is

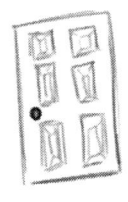

এটা দরজা
[ay-ta dhor-jah]
This, the door

এটা চাবি
[ay-ta cha-bi]
This, the key

এটা বাসা
[ay-ta bah-sha]
This, the home/house

এটা মসজিদ
[ay-ta mash-jid]
This, the mosque

এটা টেবিল
[ay-ta teh-bill]
This, the table

এটা চেয়ার
[ay-ta cheh-ar]
This, the chair

এটা ঘড়ি
[ay-ta gho-ri]
This, the clock

এটা গাড়ি
[ay-ta gha-ri]
This, the car

Exercise 3.0

এটা কি?
[ay-ta ki]

This, what?

এটা কি?
This, what?

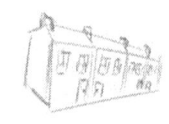

এটা বাসা।
This, the house.

এটা কি?
This, what?

এটা চেয়ার।
This, the chair.

এটা কি?
This, what?

এটা ঘড়ি।
This, the clock.

এটা কি?
This, what?

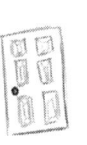

এটা দরজা।
This, the door.

Let us learn the Bengali word for "That". Thus to refer to an object at a distance, rather than in close proximity.

Bengali word	ওটা
Phoneme/s	"O" + "Tah"
Partial transliteration (underlined & Bold)	**oi**ntment + **ta**n
Transliteration	oy-ta
Translation	that / that is

ওটা গাড়ি
[oy-ta gha-ri]
That, car

ওটা চাবি
[oy-ta cha-bi]
That, key

ওটা গাছ
[oy-ta gha-ch]
That, tree

ওটা পানি
[oy-ta pani]
That, water

ওটা দুধ
[oy-ta dhoo-dh]
That, milk

ওটা চিনি
[oy-ta chi-ni]
That, sugar

ওটা লবণ
[oy-ta loh-bon]
That, salt

ওটা গোলমরিচ
[oy-ta ghool-morish]
That, black pepper

Exercise 3.1

ওটা কি?
[oy-ta ki]
That, what?

ওটা কি?
That, what?

ওটা বাসা।
That, the house.

ওটা কি?
That, what?

ওটা চেয়ার।
That, the chair.

ওটা কি?
That, what?

ওটা ঘড়ি।
That, the clock.

ওটা কি?
That, what?

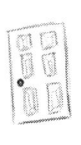

ওটা দরজা।
That, the door.

New words
নতুন শব্দ

Bangla word	Translation	Transliteration
এটা [1]	This	*ay-ta*
ওটা [2]	That	*oy-ta*
দরজা	Door	*dhorjah*
চাবি	Key	*chabi*
বাসা [3] [4]	Home/House	*bahsha*
মসজিদ	Mosque	*mashjid*
টেবিল	Table	*tehbill*
চেয়ার	Chair	*chear*
ঘড়ি	Watch	*ghori*
গাড়ি	Car	*ghari*
গাছ	Tree	*ghach*
পানি	Water	*pani*
দুধ	Milk	*dhoodh*
চিনি	Sugar	*chini*
লবণ	Salt	*loh-bon*
গোলমরিচ	Black pepper	*ghool-morish*

[1] The reader can informally refer to this word as এই [a]
[2] The reader can informally refer to this word as ও [o]
[3] বাসা is the formal word used to refer to one's home. In Bengali spoken language, however, home can be referred to also as ঘর [ghor] and বাড়ি [bah-ri]. Both refer to the individual, free-standing property/building.
[4] While বাসা, বাড়ি and ঘর are all synonymously used for one's home, গ্রাম [graam] is another term which refers to one's home but used specifically to refer to an estate or village. As opposed to the free-standing property/building.

Lesson 4.0 – Adjectives

Sometimes we are in need of describing nouns. Thus adjectives are descriptive words which allow for this. Let us introduce some Bengali adjectives.

বড় (boroh) big	**ছোট** (choo-toh) small
নতুন (noh-thoon) new	**পুরাতন** (pora-thoon) old
দুত [1] (droo-tho) fast	**ধীরে** (dhi-reh) slow
দামী (dhami) expensive	**সস্তা** [2] (shoshta) cheap

শক্তিশালী [3] (shakti-shali) strong	**দুর্বল** [4] (dhoor-bol) weak
গরম (gorom) hot	**ঠান্ডা** [5] (tanda) cold
সুন্দর [6] (shoon-dor) beautiful	**মিঠা** (me-tah) sweet

1. Consonants and graphemes দ্‌ , র and ু combine to form দু
   Hence the phoneme "droo"
2. Consonants and grapheme স্‌ , ত and া combine to form স্তা
   Hence the phoneme "sh-tha"
3. Consonants and grapheme ক্‌ , ত and ি combine to form ক্তি
   Hence the phoneme "|K|-Thi"
4. Consonants- র্‌ and ব combine to form র্ব
   Hence the phoneme "|R|-Bo"
5. Consonants and grapheme ন্‌ , ড and া combine to form ন্ডা
   Hence the phoneme "|N|-Dah"
6. Consonants ন্‌ and দ combine to form ন্দ
   Hence the phoneme "|N|-Dho"

Example 4.0
Using adjectives in sentences

এটা গাড়ি নতুন।
This car, new.
(This car is new.)

Let us introduce a Bengali conjunction to compliment the use of adjectives in sentences.

Bengali word	এবং
Phoneme/s	|AE| + Bo + Ng
Partial transliteration (underlined & Bold)	**a**ir + **bo**ard + eati**ng**
Transliteration	eh-bong
Translation	and / moreover

ওটা গাড়ি নতুন এবং দুত।
That car, new and fast.
(That car is new and fast.)

ঘর ছোট এবং মসজিদ বড়।
House, small and mosque, big.
(The house is small and the mosque is big.)

ছোট গাড়ি কোথায়?
Small car, where?
(Where is the small car?)

ছোট গাড়ী এখানে আছে।
Small car, here, there is.
(The small car is here)

হাতি বড় এবং পাখি ছোট।
Elephant, big and bird, small
(The elephant is big and the bird is small)

কোট দামী।
Coat, expensive.
(The coat is expensive.)

টেবিল দামী এবং চেয়ার সস্তা।
Table, expensive and chair, cheap.
(The table is expensive and the chair is cheap.)

চা গরম এবং দুধ ঠান্ডা।
Tea, hot and milk, hot.
(The tea is hot and milk is cold.)

ফুল সুন্দর।
Flower, beautiful.
(The flower is beautiful.)

New words
নতুন শব্দ

Bangla word	Translation	Transliteration
বড়	Big	*boroh*
ছোট	Small	*choo-toh*
নতুন	New	*noh-thoon*
পুরাতন	Old	*pora-thoon*
দুত	Fast	*droo-tho*
ধীরে	Slow	*dhi-reh*
দামী	Expensive	*dhami*
সস্তা	Cheap	*shoshta*
শক্তিশালী	Strong	*shakti-shali*
দুর্বল	Weak	*dhoor-bol*
গরম	Hot	*gorom*
ঠান্ডা	Cold	*tanda*
সুন্দর	Beautiful	*shoon-dor*
মিঠা	Sweet	*me-tah*
এবং	and / moreover [1]	*eh-bong*
এখানে	here	*eh-kaneh*
আছে	There is/That is [2]	*ah-cheh*

[1,2] Depending upon context, either translations can be utlised.

Lesson 5.0 – Adjectives- colour

রঙ
[rong]
Colour

Green
সবুজ

Red
লাল

Black
কালো

White
সাদা [1]

Yellow
হলুদ [2]

Orange
কমলা [3]

Grey
ধূসর

Gold [4]
সোনা

Pink
গোলাপী

Blue
নীল

Purple [5]
বেগুনি

Brown
বাদামী

1. synonymous in reference to both the colour and the white powder South Asian's add to their betel nut and paan.
2. synonymous in reference to both the colour and turmeric powder typically used in the Southeast Asian cuisine to create the infamous yellow colour. To traditional mehndi goers, the Gaye holud is a further reference to the use of turmeric in the Bengali tradition.
3. synonymous in reference to both the colour and the fruit
4. synonymous in reference to both the colour and the valuable metal
5. consonant- গ and grapheme- ু combine to form গু Hence the phoneme "goo"

Pronunciation of colours:

Bengali word	সবুজ
Phoneme/s	Sho + Bo + |J|
Partial transliteration (only pronounce the letters underlined & bold)	**Sho**p + **Bu**ll + **J**am
Transliteration	shobuj
Translation	Green

Bengali word	লাল
Phoneme/s	La + |L|
Partial transliteration (only pronounce the letters underlined & bold)	**La**mp + **L**amp
Transliteration	laal
Translation	Red

Bengali word	কালো
Phoneme/s	Ka + Lo
Partial transliteration (only pronounce the letters underlined & bold)	**Cu**p + **Loo**k
Transliteration	kaloo
Translation	Black

Bengali word	সাদা
Phoneme/s	Sha + Dha
Partial transliteration (only pronounce the letters underlined & bold)	**Sha**ck + **Du**ck
Transliteration	shadah
Translation	White

Bengali word	হলুদ
Phoneme/s	Ho + Lo + |DH|
Partial transliteration (only pronounce the letters underlined & bold)	**Ho**pe + **Loo**k + **D**ad
Transliteration	holud
Translation	Yellow

Bengali word	কমলা
Phoneme/s	Ko + |M| + La
Partial transliteration (only pronounce the letters underlined & bold)	**Co**p + **M**um + **La**mp
Transliteration	komla
Translation	Orange

Bengali word	ধূসর
Phoneme/s	Dho + Sho + |R|
Partial transliteration (only pronounce the letters underlined & bold)	**Do** + **Sho**p + **R**amp
Transliteration	dho-shor
Translation	Grey

Bengali word	সোনা
Phoneme/s	Sho + Na
Partial transliteration (only pronounce the letters underlined & bold)	**Sho**p + **Nu**t
Transliteration	shona
Translation	Gold

Bengali word	গোলাপী
Phoneme/s	Gho + La + Pi
Partial transliteration (only pronounce the letters underlined & bold)	**Goo**se + **La**mp + **Pea**
Transliteration	goolapi
Translation	Pink

Bengali word	নীল
Phoneme/s	Ni + |L|
Partial transliteration (only pronounce the letters underlined & bold)	**Kni**t + **L**amp
Transliteration	nil
Translation	Blue

Bengali word	বেগুনি
Phoneme/s	Beh + Go + Ni
Partial transliteration (only pronounce the letters underlined & bold)	**Bea**r + **Goo**se + **kni**t
Transliteration	beh-gooni
Translation	Purple

Bengali word	বাদামী
Phoneme/s	Ba + Dha + Mi
Partial transliteration (only pronounce the letters underlined & bold)	**Ba**n + **Da**l + **Me**
Transliteration	badami
Translation	Brown

Example 5.0
Using adjectives in sentences

নীল গাড়ি কোথায়?
Blue car, where?
(Where is the blue car?)

নীল গাড়ী এখানে আছে |
Blue car, here, there is.
(The blue car is here)

গাড়ী লাল এবং নীল হয় |
The car, red and blue, is.
(The car is red and blue.)

এটা কি?
This, what?
(What is this?)

এটা নৌকা হয় |
This, the boat, is.
(This is the boat.)

নৌকার [1] রঙ কি?
The boat's, colour, what?
(What is the boat's colour?)

নৌকার রঙ বাদামী হয় |
The boat's colour, brown, is.
(The boat's colour is brown)

কলা মিঠা এবং রঙ হলুদ হয় |
Banana, sweet and colour, yellow, is.
(The banana is sweet and its colour is yellow.)

[1] note the possessive form of the noun is achieved by adding the Bangla letter র to the end of the noun. We will cover this in more depth in the next chapter.

New words
নতুন শব্দ

Bangla word	Translation	Transliteration
রঙ	Colour	*rong*
সবুজ	Green	*shobuj*
লাল	Red	*laal*
কালো	Black	*kaloo*
সাদা	White	*shadah*
হলুদ	Yellow	*holud*
কমলা	Orange	*komla*
ধূসর	Grey	*dho-shor*
সোনা	Gold	*shona*
গোলাপী	Pink	*goolapi*
নীল	Blue	*nil*
বেগুনি	Purple	*beh-gooni*
বাদামী	Brown	*badami*
হয়	is	*hoy*

Possessive form

Bangla word	Translation	Transliteration
নৌকার	Boat's	*no-kar*

Lesson 6.0 – a Possessive form of nouns

We have introduced a number of Bengali nouns to our vocabulary. Remember, they can be names of a person, object, place etc. Nouns are very often required in its possessive form to convey a relationship between itself and another. In the English language, this is typically achieved by adding an apostrophe and the letter "S" to the end of the noun.

English Example No. 1 -

noun	Boat

Possessive form of noun	Boat's
Example sentence	The boat's colour is beautiful.

English Example No. 2 –

noun	Amelia

Possessive form of noun	Amelia's
Example sentence	Amelia's daddy is strong.

Thus in a similar fashion, and in the Bengali script, the possessive form is achieved by adding the consonant letter র [Ro] to the end of the noun in question. Reader to note the full consonant letter [Ro] is not pronounced, but rather the first letter i.e. [|R|]. Let us appreciate…

Bangla Example No. 1 –

Bangla noun	নৌকা

Possessive form of noun	নৌকার
Example sentence	নৌকার রঙ সুন্দর।
Transliteration	No-kar rong shondor.
Translation	The boat's colour is beautiful.

Bangla Example No. 2 –

Bangla noun	আমিলিয়া

Possessive form of noun	আমিলিয়ার
Example sentence	আমিলিয়ার বাবা শক্তিশালী।
Transliteration	Ameli-ar baba shakti-shali.
Translation	Amelia's daddy is strong

Bangla Example No. 3 –

Bangla noun	গাড়ি

Possessive form of noun	গাড়ির
Example sentence	গাড়ির চাবি।
Transliteration	ghari'r cha-bi
Translation	Car's key [1]

Bangla Example No. 4 –

Bangla noun	বাবা

Possessive form of noun	বাবার
Example sentence	বাবার জন্মদিন [2]।
Transliteration	baba'r jonmo-deen
Translation	Dad's birthday

Bangla Example No. 5 –

Bangla noun	নদী

Possessive form of noun	নদীর
Example sentence	নদীর পানি।
Transliteration	noh-dhi'r pani
Translation	River's water

Bangla Example No. 6 –

Bangla noun	কোট

Possessive form of noun	কোটের [3]
Example sentence	কোটের বোতাম।
Transliteration	kooteh'r bootham
Translation	Coat's button

Bangla Example No. 7 –

Bangla noun	ফুল

Possessive form of noun	ফুলের [4]
Example sentence	ফুলের পাতা।
Transliteration	fooleh'r pa-tha
Translation	Flowers leaf

Bangla Example No. 8 –

Bangla noun	গাছ

Possessive form of noun	গাছের [5]
Example sentence	গাছের পাতা।
Transliteration	gha-che'r pa-tha
Translation	Tree's leaf

1. This is a direct translation, however, the term "Car key" is more accurate.
2. consonants- ন্ and ম combine to form ন্ম
   Hence the phoneme "|N|-Mo"
3. When the Bangla noun ends with a consonant without a vowel grapheme, the possessive form of the noun will also add the grapheme ে to the last consonant [ট], as well as র.
   Thus "koot" becomes "kooteh'r"
4. A further example and similar to reference 3.
   The Bangla noun ends with a consonant without a vowel grapheme, thus the possessive form of the noun will also add the grapheme ে to the last consonant [ল], as well as র
   Thus "Fool" becomes "Fooleh'r"
5. A further example and similar to reference 3 & 4.
   The Bangla noun ends with a consonant without a vowel grapheme, thus the possessive form of the noun can also add the grapheme ে to the last consonant [ছ], as well as র
   Thus "ghach" becomes "ghache'r"

Example 6.0
Using the possessive form of nouns in sentences

গাড়ির চাবি কোথায়?
The car's key, where?
(Where is the car key?)

গাড়ির চাবি এখানে আছে ।
The car keys, here, there is.
(The car key is here)

বাবার জন্মদিন আজ?
Dad's birthday, today?
(Is it dad's birthday today?)

না ।
বাবার জন্মদিন আগামীকাল ।
No. Dad's birthday, tomorrow.
(No. Dad's birthday is tomorrow.)

মায়ের জন্মদিন আজ
Mum's birthday, today?
(Is it mum's birthday today?)

হাঁ ।
মায়ের জন্মদিন আজ ।
Yes. Mum's birthday, today.
(Yes. Mum's birthday is today.)

ফুলের পাতা রঙ সবুজ
Flower's leaf, colour, green.
(The flower's leaf colour is green.)

কলা গাছের রঙ কি?
Banana tree's colour, what?
(What is the banana tree's colour?)

কলা গাছের রঙ সবুজ এবং হলুদ ।
Banana tree's colour, green and yellow.
(The banana tree's colour is green and yellow.)

আম গাছের রঙ কি?
Mango tree's colour, what?
(What is the mango tree's colour?)

আম গাছের রঙ সবুজ এবং কমলা ।
Mango tree's colour, green and orange.
(The mango tree's colour is green and orange.)

নদীর পানি ঠান্ডা হয় ।
River's water, cold, is.
(The river's water is cold)

কোটের বোতাম দামী হয় ।
Coat's button, expensive, is.
(The coat's button is expensive.)

এই ছোট বইয়ের রঙ কি?
This, small book's colour, what?
(What is this small book's colour?)

ছোট বইয়ের রঙ বেগুনি ।
Small book's colour, purple.
(The small book's colour is purple.)

বলের রঙ কি?
Ball's colour, what?
(What is the colour of the ball?)

বলের রঙ সাদা ।
Ball's colour, white.
(The ball's colour is white)

New words
নতুন শব্দ

Bangla word	Translation	Transliteration
আমিলিয়া	Amelia	*ameli-ah*
বাবা	Dad (Daddy)	*baba*
জন্মদিন	Birthday	*jonmo-deen*
পাতা	Leaf	*patha*
না	No	*nah*
হাঁ	Yes	*hah*
আজ	Today	*aj*
আগামীকাল	Tomorrow	*ah-ghami-kayl*

Possessive form

Bangla word	Translation	Transliteration
আমিলিয়ার	Amelia's	*ameli-ar*
গাড়ির	Car's	*ghari'r*
বাবার	Dad's	*baba'r*
নদীর	River's	*noh-dhi'r*
কোটের	Coat's	*kooteh'r*
ফুলের	Flower's	*fooleh'r*
গাছের	Tree's	*gha-che'r*
মায়ের	Mum's	*ma-er*
বইয়ের	Book's	*boi-er*
বলের	Ball's	*bol-ler*

Lesson 7.0 – Numbers. 1-10

সংখ্যার
[shong-har]
Numberss

English No.	Bangla No.	Bangla word	Phoneme
1	১	এক	eh-|k|
2	২	দুই	dho-|E|
3	৩	তিন	thi-|N|
4	৪	চার	cha-|R|
5	৫	পাঁচ	pa-|CH|
6	৬	ছয়	cho-|E|
7	৭	সাত	sha-|TH|
8	৮	আট	ah-|T|
9	৯	নয়	no-|E|
10	১০	দশ	dho-|SH|

First Consonant	Second Consonant	Bangla word	Partial transliteration
এ	ক	এক	**e**gg + **k**ick

(ek) – One

First Consonant	Second Consonant	Bangla word	Partial transliteration
দ	ই	দুই	**do** + **ea**gle

(dhoi) – Two

First Consonant	Second Consonant	Bangla word	Partial transliteration
ত	ন	তিন	**thi**ck + **n**ut

(theen) – Three

First Consonant	Second Consonant	Bangla word	Partial transliteration
চ	র	চার	**chu**ck + **r**amp

(chaar) – Four

First Consonant	Second Consonant	Bangla word	Partial transliteration
প	চ	পাঁচ	**pa**rk+ **ch**uck

(pasch) – Five

First Consonant	Second Consonant	Bangla word	Partial transliteration
ছ	য়	ছয়	**cho**p + **ea**gle

(choy) – Six

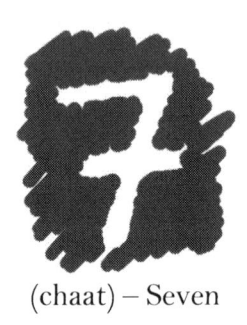

First Consonant	Second Consonant	Bangla word	Partial transliteration
স	ত	সাত	<u>shu</u>t+ <u>t</u>ree

(chaat) – Seven

First Consonant	Second Consonant	Bangla word	Partial transliteration
আ	ট	আট	<u>a</u>rt + <u>t</u>ree

(aht) – Eight

First Consonant	Second Consonant	Bangla word	Partial transliteration
ন	য়	নয়	**kn**ock+ **ea**gle

(noy) – Nine

First Consonant	Second Consonant	Bangla word	Partial transliteration
দ	শ	দশ	**dho**ti + shu**sh**

(dhosh) – Ten

Example 7.0
Using numbers in sentences

এখানে কতগুলো কলা আছে?
Here, how many, banana, there is?
(How many bananas are there here?)

এখানে ছয় কলা আছে।
Here, six banana, there is.
(There are six bananas here.)

সেখানে কতগুলো আম আছে?
There, how many, mango, there is.
(How many mangos, are there, there?)

সেখানে দশ আম আছে।
There, ten mangos, there is.
(There are ten mangos there.)

এখন কটা বাজে?
Now, how much, time?
(What is the time now?)

এখন একটা বাজে।
Now, one o'clock.
(It is one o'clock now.)

ধন্যবাদ।
Thank you.
(Thank you.)

এটা কি?
This, what?
(What is this?)

এটা বই |
This, book
(This is a book)

বই কত টাকা?
The book, how many, taka?
(How much is the book?)

বই সাত টাকা |
The book, eight taka.
(The book is eight taka)

ধন্যবাদ চাচা |
Thank you, uncle.
(Thank you, uncle.)

ঠিক আছে |
Right, that is.
(OK.)

New words
নতুন শব্দ

Bangla word	Translation	Transliteration
দুই	Two	*dhoi*
তিন	Three	*theen*
চার	Four	*chaar*
পাঁচ	Five	*pasch*
ছয়	Six	*choy*
সাত	Seven	*chaat*
আট	Eight	*aht*
নয়	Nine	*noy*
দশ	Ten	*dhosh*
কতগুলো	How many?	*kotho-gholoo*
সেখানে	There	*sheh-kaneh*
এখন	Now	*eh-kon*
কৈঢা	How much?	*kota*
বাজে	*	*bajeh*
ধন্যবাদ	Thank you	*dhonya-baadh*
কত	How many?	*kotho*
টাকা [1]	Taka / Money	*taka*
চাচা	Uncle	*chacha*
ঠিক	right	*teek*
ঠিক আছে	OK	*teek-acheh*

[1] In Bengali, the word taka is synonymous with the word, money. Thus taka can be used in reference to the unit of exchange i.e. taka (currency) but also the principle of money itself.

*Translation can vary thus depending upon context. When asking for the time, it refers to the hour of the day.

Lesson 8.0 – Pronouns

সর্বনাম
[shor-bo nam]
Pronouns

A pronoun replaces a noun in a sentence, making the subject a person or a thing. Thus it can function as a noun phrase and refers either to participants in a dialogue or to someone or something mentioned elsewhere.

Bengali pronouns are very important because their structure is used in everyday conversation. The more you use it, the closer you come to mastering the Bengali language.

<u>Dealing with participants in a conversation</u>

আমি	তুমি [1]	আমরা
[ah-mi]	[tho-mi]	[amo-rah]
i	you	we

আমাকে	তোমাকে
[ah-ma-keh]	[tho-ma-keh]
me	You

[1] Alternatively, আপনি can be used. [ah-po-ni]. This is the more formal word used towards someone older and of respect.

The pronouns above are referred to as personal pronouns. They are not gender sensitive thus applicable to both male and female. Thus referring to the persons speaking, the persons spoken to or the persons or things spoken about.

Dealing with non-participants in a conversation

সে	তারা
[shey]	[tha-ra]
he/she/it	they

তাকে	সেগুলো
[tha-keh]	[shey-gho-loo]
him/her	those

Thus the pronouns above are used to refer to individuals/objects external to the dialogue taking place.

Example 8.0
Dealing with participants in a conversation

আমি সাকিব । তুমি সাবির । আমরা ভাই ।
I, Sakib. You, Sabir. We, brothers.
(I am Sakib. You are Sabir. We are brothers.)

আমি সাবির ।
I, Sabir.
(I am Sabir.)

তুমি জাকিয়া এবং তুমি তানিয়া ।
You, Zakiyah and you, Taniyah.
(You are Zakiyah and you are Taniyah)

আমরা ভাই এবং বোন । আমরাও ছাত্র ।
We, brothers and sisters. We, also, students.
(We are brothers and sisters. We are also students.)

তুমি কে?
You, who?
(Who are you?)

আমি মারিয়া ।
I, Mariyah.
(I am Mariyah)

আমি তানিয়া বোনের ছোট বোন ।
I, Taniyah afa's, small, sister.
(I am Taniyah afa's younger sister)

বাবা আমি তোমাকে ভালোবাসি ।
Daddy, I, you, love.
(Daddy, I love you.)

Example 8.1
Dealing with non-participants in a conversation

কোথায় সাকিব আছে?
Where, Sakib, there is?
(Where is Sakib?)

সে এখানে।
He, here.
(He is here.)

এবং কোথায় মারিয়া আছে?
And where, Mariyah, there is?
(And where is Mariyah?)

সে সেখানে।
She, there.
(She is there.)

তারা কি করছে?
They, what, is doing?
(What are they doing?)

তারা বই পড়ছে।
They, book, reading.
(They are reading books.)

তারা ঠিক আছে?
They, okay?
(Are they okay?)

হাঁ তারা ঠিক আছে।
Yes, okay.
(Yes, they are okay)

New words
নতুন শব্দ

Bangla word	Translation	Transliteration
আমি	I	*ah-mi*
তুমি / আপনি	You	*tho-mi/ah-po-ni*
আমরা	We	*amo-rah*
আমাকে	Me	*ah-ma-keh*
তোমাকে	You	*tho-ma-keh*
সে	He / She / It	*shey*
তারা	They	*tha-ra*
তাকে	Him / Her	*tha-keh*
সেগুলো	Those	*shey-gho-loo*
ভাই	Brother / Brothers	*bai*
বোন	Sister / Sisters	*boyn*
আমরাও	We are also	*amo-rah-o*
ছাত্র [1]	Student / Students	*chat-tro*
কোথায়	Where?	*koo-thay*
করছে	Is doing	*koroh-cheh*

1 Consonants ত and র combine to form ত্র
   Hence the phoneme "|Th| - ro"

Possessive form

Bangla word	Translation	Transliteration
বোনের	Sister's	*bo-ner*

Proper nouns

Bangla word	Translation	Transliteration
সাকিব	Sakib	*shakib*
সাবির	Sabir	*shabir*
জাকিয়া	Zakiyah	*jakia*
তানিয়া	Taniyah	*thania*
মারিয়া	Mariyah	*maria*

Verbs

Bangla word	Translation	Transliteration
ভালোবাসি	Love	*balo-bashi*
পড়ছে	Reading	*poroh-che*

Lesson 9.0 – Possessive Pronouns

Possessive pronouns are pronouns that demonstrate ownership.

<u>Deal with participants in a conversation</u>

আমার	তোমার [1]	আমাদের
[ah-mar]	[too-mar]	[ama-dhe-|r|]
my	your	us /our

[1] Alternatively, আপনার can be used. [Ah-po-na-|R|]. This is the more formal word used towards someone older and of respect.

<u>Deal with non-participants in a conversation</u>

তার	তাদের
[tha-|r|]	[tha-ha-deh-|R|]
his/her	their

Example 9.0
Deal with participants in a conversation

তোমার নাম কি?
Your, name, what?
(What is your name?)

আমার নাম আবদুল।
My name, Abdul.
(My name is Abdul.)

তুমি কে?
You, who?
(Who are you?)

আমি তোমার বাবা।
I, your, Dad.
(I am your Dad.)

আপনার বাড়ি কোথায়?
Your home, where?
(Where is your home?)

আমাদের বাড়ি সিলেট, বাংলাদেশ।
Our home, Sylhet, Bangladesh.
(Our home is in Sylhet, Bangladesh.)

আপনার গ্রাম কোথায়?
Your village, where?
(Where is your village?)

আমাদের গ্রাম বালাগঞ্জ।
Our village, Balagonj.
(Our village is Balagonj.)

বাবা আপনার জন্মদিন কবে?
Dad, your, birthday, when?
(Dad when is your birthday?)

আমার জন্মদিন আজ হয় ।
My birthday, today, is.
(My birthday is today)

শুভ জন্মদিন বাবা
Happy birthday, Dad.
(Happy birthday Dad.)

Example 9.1
Deal with non-participants in a conversation

সে কে?
He, who?
(Who is he?)

সে আমার ভাই |
He, my, brother.
(He is my brother.)

তার নাম কি?
His, name, what?
(What is his name?)

তার নাম দিনার |
His name, Dinar.
(His name is Dinar.)

তার কত ছেলে এবং মেয়ে আছে?
His, how many, sons and daughters, there is?
(How many sons and daughters does he have?)

তার দুই ছেলে এবং তিন মেয়ে আছে |
His, one son and one daughter, there is.
(He got one son and one daughter.)

তার ছেলের নাম কি?
His son's name, what?
(What are the name of his son's?)

তার ছেলের নাম ইমতিয়াজ এবং ইশতিয়াক |
His son's name, Imtiaz and Ishtiaq.
(His son's name is Imitiaz and Ishtiaq.)

ইমতিয়াজ বড় হয় |
Imtiyaaz, big, is.
(Imtiyaaz is the eldest)

তার মেয়েদের নাম কি?
His daughter's name, what?
(What are the name of his daughter's?)

তার মেয়েদের নাম তাসিন আবিদা এবং জুবাইদা ।
His daughter's name, Tasin, Abida and Zubaida.
(His daughter's names are Tasin, Abida and Zubaida.)

তাসিন সব বড় হয় ।
Tasin, all, big, is.
(Tasin is the eldest)

জুবাইদা সব ছোট হয় ।
Zubaida, all, small, is.
(Zubaida is the youngest)

তাদের পরিবার বড় হয় ।
Their family, big, is.
(Their family is big.)

তাদের গাড়ি আছে?
Their, car, there is?
(They have a car?)

হাঁ তাদের গাড়ি আছে ।
Yes, their, car, there is.
(Yes. They have a car.)

গাড়ি খুব বড় ।
Car, very, big.
(The car is very big)

তার জন্মদিন কবে?
His, birthday, when?
(When is his birthday?)

তার জন্মদিন আজ।
His birthday, today.
(His birthday is today)

New words
নতুন শব্দ

Bangla word	Translation	Transliteration
আমার	My	*amar*
তোমার / আপনার	Your	*tomar/apohnar*
আমাদের	Us / Our	*amah-der*
তার	His / Her	*tha-ra*
তাদের	Their	*tha-der*
নাম	Name	*nam*
বাড়ি	House / Home	*bari*
গ্রাম	Village	*graam*
জন্মদিন	Birthday	*jonma-din*
কবে	When?	*kobeh*
শুভ	Happy	*shoo-boh*
শুভ জন্মদিন	Happy Birthday!	*shoo-boh jonma-din*
ছেলে	Son	*che-leh*
মেয়ে	Daughter	*meh-eh*
সব	All / Everything	*shob*

Possessive form

Bangla word	Translation	Transliteration
ছেলের	Son's	*che-ler*
মেয়েদের	Daughter's	*meh-eh-der*

Proper nouns

Bangla word	Translation	Transliteration
আবদুল	Abdul	*abdul*
দিনার	Dinar	*dinar*
ইমতিয়াজ	Imtiyaaz	*imti-az*
ইশতিয়াক	Ishtiaq	*ishti-aq*
তাসিন	Tasin	*tasin*
আবিদা	Abida	*abida*
জুবাইদা	Zubaida	*zubay-da*
সিলেট	Sylhet	*shi-let*
বাংলাদেশ	Bangladesh	*bangladesh*
বালাগঞ্জ	Balagonj	*balagonj*

Adverb

Bangla word	Translation	Transliteration
খুব	Very	*khoob*

Lesson 10.0 – Forming words. Proper nouns

Proper nouns are nouns that are names used for individual persons, organisations, places etc. Examples being Amelia, Samsung and London, respectively. A big hint being the initial capital letter. Let us now introduce proper nouns in the Bengali script.

Note the word "Bengali" is a proper noun in itself.

We will look at three specific categories of proper nouns to help the reader form useful, complete sentences.
1. Countries
2. Days
3. Names

Countries

দেশ
[desh]
Country/s

There are almost 200 countries in the world today. So let us avoid listing through them all and introduce few.

Country in English	Country in Bengali	Transliteration
Bangladesh	বাংলাদেশ	*bangladesh*
England	ইংল্যান্ড	*england*
America	আমেরিকা	*ah-merica*
Italy	ইতালি	*ithaly*
Canada	কানাডা	*kanada*
Japan	জাপান	*japan*
Russia	রাশিয়া	*rashia*
Iran	ইরান	*iran*
Iraq	ইরাক	*irak*
Qatar	কাতার	*katar*
Pakistan	পাকিস্তান	*pakistan*
Panama	পানামা	*panama*
Kenya	কেনিয়া	*keny-ah*
Peru	পেরু	*peru*
Saudi Arabia	সৌদি আরব	*shodhi-arab*
Greece	গ্রীস	*greesh*

Example 10.0

য়নব আপনি কোন দেশ থেকেন?
Zaynab, you, which, country, from?
(Zaynab, which country are you from?)

আমি বাংলাদেশ থেকে।
I, Bangladesh, from.
(I am from Bangladesh.)

আপনার ঠিকানা কি?
Your, address, what?
(What is your address?)

আমার ঠিকানা বালাগঞ্জ, সিলেট।
My address, Balagonj, Sylhet.
(My address is Balagonj, Sylhet.)

বাংলাদেশের রাজধানী কি?
Bangladesh's capital, what?
(What is Bangladesh's capital?)

বাংলাদেশের রাজধানী ঢাকা।
Bangladesh's capital, Dhaka.
(Bangladesh's capital is Dhaka.)

টনি আপনি কোন দেশ থেকেন?
Tony, you, which, country, from?
(Tony, which country are you from?)

আমি ইংল্যান্ড থেকে।
I, England, from.
(I am from England.)

ইংল্যান্ডের রাজধানী কি?
England's capital, what?
(What is England's capital?)

ইংল্যান্ডের রাজধানী লন্ডন ।
England's capital, London.
(England's capital is London.)

দেশের আইন কঠিন ।
Country's law, difficult.
(The country's law is difficult.)

হাসান আপনি কোন দেশ থেকেন?
Hasan, you, which, country, from?
(Hasan, which country are you from?)

আমি ইরাক থেকে ।
I, Iraq, from.
(I am from Iraq.)

ইরাকের রাজধানী কি?
Iraq's capital, what?
(What is Iraq's capital?)

ইরাকের রাজধানী বাগদাদ ।
Iraq's capital, Baghdad.
(Iraq's capital is Baghdad.)

আকিরা আপনি কোন দেশ থেকেন?
Akira, you, which, country, from?
(Akira, which country are you from?)

আমি জাপান থেকে ।
I, Japan, from.
(I am from Japan.)

জাপানের রাজধানী কি?
Japan's capital, what?
(What is Japan's capital?)

জাপানের রাজধানী টোকিও ।
Japan's capital, Tokyo.
(Japan's capital is Tokyo.)

কত মহাদেশ আছে?
How many, Continents, there is?
(How many continents are there?)

সাত মহাদেশ আছে।
Seven, continents, there is.
(There are seven continents.)

কোন মহাদেশে বাংলাদেশ হয়?
Which, on the continent, Bangladesh, is?
(On which continent is Bangladesh?)

বাংলাদেশ এশিয়াতে [1] ।
Bangladesh, in Asia.
(Bangladesh is in Asia.)

কোন মহাদেশে ইংল্যান্ড হয়?
Which, on the continent, England, is?
(On which continent is England?)

ইংল্যান্ড ইউরোপে [2] ।
England, in Europe.
(England is in Europe.)

---

[1] Asia in Bengali is referred to as এশিয়া

Note the grapheme ে and consonant ত is applied to the end of the work to incorporate the noun "in".

[2] Europe in Bengali is referred to as ইউরোপ

Note the grapheme ে is applied to the last consonant to incorporate the noun "in".

New words
নতুন শব্দ

Bangla word	Translation	Transliteration
কোন	Which?	*koon*
দেশ	Country	*desh*
থেকে *	From	*the-keh*
কঠিন	Difficult	*ko-tin*
রাজধানী	Capital (city)	*raj-dhah-ni*
মহাদেশ	Continents	*maha-desh*

*Referred to as **থেকেন** when asking question to person directly. Thus not used in 3rd person conversations.

Possessive form

Bangla word	Translation	Transliteration
এশিয়াতে	In Asia	*eh-shia-teh*
ইউরোপে	In Europe	*eo-ro-peh*

Proper nouns

Bangla word	Translation	Transliteration
ইংল্যান্ড	England	*england*
আমেরিকা	America	*ah-merica*
ইতালি	Italy	*ithaly*
কানাডা	Canada	*kanada*
জাপান	Japan	*japan*
রাশিয়া	Russia	*rashia*
ইরান	Iran	*iran*
ইরাক	Iraq	*irak*

কাতার	Qatar	*katar*
পাকিস্তান	Pakistan	*pakistan*
পানামা	Panama	*panama*
কেনিয়া	Kenya	*keny-ah*
পেরু	Peru	*peru*
সৌদি আরব	Saudi Arabia	*shodhi-arab*
গ্রীস	Greece	*greesh*
এশিয়া	Asia	*eh-shia*
ইউরোপ	Europe	*eo-rop*
ঢাকা	Dhaka	*daka*
লন্ডন	London	*london*
টোকিও	Tokyo	*toh-kio*
য়নব	Zaynab	*zaynab*
টনি	Tony	*tony*
হাসান	Hasan	*hasan*
আকিরা	Akira	*akira*

Days of the week

দিন
[dhin]
Day/s

Day in English	Day in Bengali	Transliteration
Monday	সোমবার	shom-bar
Tuesday	মঙ্গলবার [1]	mong-gol-bar
Wednesday	বুধবার	budh-bar
Thursday	বৃহস্পতিবার [2]	bri-hosh-poti-bar
Friday	শুক্রবার [3]	shu-kro-bar
Saturday	শনিবার	sho-ni-bar
Sunday	রবিবার	ro-bi-bar

1 Individual letters sometimes combine to form a shorthand version. These shorthand versions can very easily trip the whisky reader however if you break these shorthands to individual units, all makes sense. Let us analyze!

Bangla word	মঙ্গলবার
Bangla letters	ম ঙ গ ল বা র
Phoneme	**mo + ng + go +|L| + ba + |R|**

Thus ঙ + গ combine to form ঙ্গ

2 Similar to the Bengali letters grouped in the word Tuesday, Wednesday has something similar.

Bangla word	বৃহস্পতিবার
Bangla letters	বৃ হ স্ প তি বা র
Phoneme	bri + ho + sh + po + thi + ba + |R|

Thus স্ + প combine to form স্প

3 The Bengali word for Friday groups two sets of letters.

Bangla word	শুক্রবার
Bangla letters	শ ু ক্ র বা র
Phoneme	sho + |K| + ro + ba + |R|

Note ু is the diacritic form of উ. Refer to table 2.1.

Thus শ + ু combine to form শু

Thus ক্ + র combine to form ক্র

Exercise 10.1

গতকাল | আজ | আগামীকাল
Yesterday | Today | Tomorrow

আজ সোমবার | আগামীকাল কি বার?
Today, Monday. Tomorrow, what day?
(Today is Monday. What day is tomorrow?)

আগামীকাল মঙ্গলবার হয় |
Tomorrow, Tuesday, is.
(Tomorrow is Tuesday)

ঠিক আছে |
Right, that is.
(OK.)

গতকাল রবিবার ছিল |
Yesterday, Sunday was.

আমিনা আগামীকাল কি দিন?
Amina, tomorrow, what, day?
(Amina, what day is tomorrow?)

আগামীকাল শনিবার হয় |
Tomorrow, Saturday, is.
(Tomorrow is Saturday)

New words
নতুন শব্দ

Bangla word	Translation	Transliteration
গতকাল	Yesterday	gho-tho-kayl
বার	Day / Time	barr
ছিল	Was	chilo
দিন	Day	dhin

Proper nouns

সোমবার	Monday	shom-bar
মঙ্গলবার	Tuesday	mong-gol-bar
বুধবার	Wednesday	budh-bar
বৃহস্পতিবার	Thursday	bri-hosh-poti-bar
শুক্রবার	Friday	shu-kro-bar
শনিবার	Saturday	sho-ni-bar
রবিবার	Sunday	ro-bi-bar
আমিনা	Amina	amina

Names

নাম

[nam]
Name/s

Name in English	Names in Bengali	Transliteration
Abbie	আবিহ	*abbie*
Abdul	আবদুল	*abdul*
Abida	আবিদা	*abida*
Aki	আকি	*aki*
Akira	আকিরা	*akira*
Amelia	আমিলিয়া	*amelia*
Amina	আমিনা	*amina*
Daniel	ড্যানিয়েল	*daniel*
Dian	ডিয়ান	*dian*
Dinar	দিনার	*dinar*
Fatima	ফাতিমা	*fathima*
Fawziyah	ফাওজিয়া	*fawjiya*
Hasan	হাসান	*hashan*
Hazera	হাজেরা	*hajerah*
Imtiaz	ইমতিয়াজ	*imtiaaj*
Ishtiaq	ইশতিয়াক	*ishtiak*
Jahangir	জাহাঙ্গীর	*jahang-gir*
Kajol	কাজল	*ka-jol*
Karima	কারিমা	*karima*
Lipa	লিপা	*lipa*
Mariyah	মারিয়া	*maria*
Muhammad	মুহাম্মদ	*mohammadh*

Nahian	নাহিয়ান	*nahiyaan*
Naimah	নাঈমা	*naimah*
Omaya	ওমায়া	*omaya*
Opey	অপি	*opi*
Osama	ওসামা	*osama*
Sabir	সাবির	*shabir*
Sabirah	সাবিরা	*shabira*
Sakib	সাকিব	*shakib*
Samina	সামিনা	*shamina*
Tamim	তামিম	*thamim*
Tamanna	তামান্না	*thamanna*
Taniyah	তানিয়া	*thania*
Tasin	তাসিন	*thashin*
Tasnim	তাসনিম	*tashnim*
Tony	টনি	*tony*
Zakiyah	জাকিয়া	*jakiya*
Zaynab	য়নব	*jaynab*
Zubaida	জুবাইদা	*jobaydha*

Example 10.2

আপনার নাম কি?
Your name what?
(What is your name?)

আমার নাম সামিনা ।
My name, Samina.
(My name is Samina)

আপনার ডাকনাম কি?
Your surname, what?
(What is your surname?)

আমার ডাকনাম বেগম ।
My surname, Begum.
(My surname is Begum.)

আমার পুরো নাম মোহাম্মাদ আবদুল । আপনার পুরো নাম কি?
My full name, Muhammad Abdul. Your full name, what?
(My name is Muhammad Abdul. What is your full name?)

আমার পুরো নাম আমিনা বিবি ।
My full name, Amina Bibi.
(My full name is Amina Bibi.)

আমিনা আপনার বাবার নাম কি?
Amina, your, father's name, what?
(Amina, what is your father's name?)

আমার বাবার নাম নুরুল হক।
My father's name, Nurul Haque.
(My father's name is Nurul Haque.)

আপনার মায়ের নাম কি?
You, mother's name, what?
(What is your mother's name?)

আমার মায়ের নাম জাহানারা বেগম।
My mother's name, Jahanara Begum.
(My mother's name is Jahanara Begum.)

New words
নতুন শব্দ

Bangla word	Translation	Transliteration
Surname	ডাকনাম	*dak-nam*
Full	পুরো	*poo-ro*

Possessive form

Bangla word	Translation	Transliteration
Mother's	মায়েরা	*ma-er*

Proper nouns

Bangla word	Translation	Transliteration
Abbie	আবিহ	*abbie*
Aki	আকি	*aki*
Daniel	ড্যানিয়েল	*daniel*
Dian	ডিয়ান	*dian*
Fatima	ফাতিমা	*fathima*
Fawziyah	ফাওজিয়া	*fawjiya*
Hazera	হাজেরা	*hajerah*
Jahangir	জাহাঙ্গীর	*jahang-gir*
Kajol	কাজল	*ka-jol*
Karima	কারিমা	*karima*
Lipa	লিপা	*lipa*
Muhammad	মোহাম্মাদ	*mohammadh*
Nahian	নাহিয়ান	*nahiyaan*
Naimah	নাঈমা	*naimah*
Omaya	ওমায়া	*omaya*
Opey	অপি	*opi*

Osama	ওসামা	*osama*
Sabirah	সাবিরা	*shabira*
Samina	সামিনা	*shamina*
Tamim	তামিম	*thamim*
Tamanna	তামান্না	*thamanna*
Tasnim	তাসনিম	*tashnim*
Begum	বেগম	*beh-gom*
Bibi	বিবি	*bee-bee*
Nurul	নুরুল	*noo-rool*
Haque	হক	*hawk*
Jahanara	জাহানারা	*jahanara*

Lesson 11.0 – Numbers. 1-100

সংখ্যার
[shong-har]
Numbers

Bangla No.	Bangla word	Phoneme	Transliteration
০	শূন্য	shoon-noh	*shoonoh*
১	এক	eh-|k|	*ek*
২	দুই	dho-|E|	*doi*
৩	তিন	thi-|N|	*theen*
৪	চার	cha-|R|	*chaar*
৫	পাঁচ	pa-|CH|	*pasch*
৬	ছয়	cho-|E|	*choy*
৭	সাত	sha-|TH|	*shat*
৮	আট	ah-|T|	*aht*
৯	নয়	no-|E|	*noy*

১০	দশ	dho-|SH|	*dhosh*
১১	এগারো	eh-gha-ro	*eh-garo*
১২	বারো	ba-ro	*baro*
১৩	তেরো	theh-ro	*tero*
১৪	চৌদ্দ [1]	cho-|DH|-dho	*choddo*
১৫	পনেরো	po-neh-ro	*ponero*
১৬	ষোলো	sho-loh	*shollo*
১৭	সতেরো	sho-theh-ro	*shotero*
১৮	আঠারো	ah-ta-ro	*ataro*
১৯	উনিশ	oo-ni-|SH|	*onnish*

২০	বিশ 2	bi-|SH|	*bish*
২১	একুশ	eh-ko-|SH|	*ekosh*
২২	বাইশ	ba-|E|-|SH|	*baesh*
২৩	তেইশ	theh-|E|-|SH|	*theh-esh*
২৪	চব্বিশ	cho-|B|-bi-|SH|	*chobbish*
২৫	পঁচিশ	po-chi-|SH|	*pochish*
২৬	ছাব্বিশ	sha-bi-|SH|	*chabbish*
২৭	সাতাশ	sha-tha-|SH|	*shatha-esh*
২৮	আটাশ	ah-ta-|SH|	*ata-esh*
২৯	ঊনত্রিশ	oo-|N|-tri-|SH|	*ontrish*

৩০	ত্রিশ	tri-|SH|	*trish*
৩১	একত্রিশ	eh-|K|-tri-|SH|	*ek-trish*
৩২	বত্রিশ	bo-tri-|SH|	*bot-trish*
৩৩	তেত্রিশ	theh-tri-|SH|	*thet-trish*
৩৪	চৌত্রিশ	chou-tri-|SH	*chow-trish*
৩৫	পঁয়ত্রিশ	pi-|E|-tri-|SH|	*pie-trish*
৩৬	ছত্রিশ	cho-tri-|SH|	*cho-trish*
৩৭	সাঁইত্রিশ	|SH|-|E|-tri-|SH|	*shy-trish*
৩৮	আটত্রিশ	ah-|T|-tri-|SH|	*at-trish*
৩৯	ঊনচল্লিশ 3	oo-no-cho-|L|-li-|SH|	*onno-chollish*

৪০	চল্লিশ	cho-|L|-li-|SH|	*chollish*
৪১	একচল্লিশ	eh-|K|-cho-|L|-li-|SH|	*ek-chollish*
৪২	বিয়াল্লিশ	be-ah-|L|-li-|SH|	*beh-allish*
৪৩	তেতাল্লিশ	theh-tha-|L|-li-|SH|	*theh-thallish*
৪৪	চুয়াল্লিশ	cho-ah-|L|-li-|SH|	*cho-allish*
৪৫	পঁয়তাল্লিশ	pi-|E|-tha-|L|-li-|SH|	*pie-thallish*
৪৬	ছেচল্লিশ	che-cho-|L|-li-|SH|	*cheh-chollish*
৪৭	সাতচল্লিশ	sha-|TH|-cho-|L|-li-|SH|	*shat-chollish*
৪৮	আটচল্লিশ	ah-|T|-cho-|L|-li-|SH|	*at-chollish*
৪৯	ঊনপঞ্চাশ [4]	Ooh-no-po-|N|-cha-|SH|	*ono-ponchash*

৫০	পঞ্চাশ	po-|N|-cha-|SH|	*ponchash*
৫১	একান্ন [5]	eh-ka-|N|-no	*ekanno*
৫২	বায়ান্ন	ba-ah-|N|-no	*ba-anno*
৫৩	তিপ্পান্ন [6]	thi-|P|-pa-|N|-no	*thi-panno*
৫৪	চুয়ান্ন	cho-ah-|N|-no	*cho-anno*

৫৫	পঞ্চান্ন	Po-|N|-cha-|N|-no	ponchanno
৫৬	ছাপ্পান্ন	cha-|P|-pa-|N|-no	chappanno
৫৭	সাতান্ন	sha-tha-|N|-no	shathanno
৫৮	আটান্ন	ah-ta-|N|-no	atanno
৫৯	ঊনষাট	oh-no-sha-|T|	ono-shyte

৬০	ষাট	sha-|T|	shayte
৬১	একষট্টি [7]	eh-|K|-sho-|T|-ti	ek-shotti
৬২	বাষট্টি	ba-sho-|T|-ti	ba-shotti
৬৩	তেষট্টি	theh-sho-|T|-ti	theh-shotti
৬৪	চৌষট্টি	cho-sho-|T|-ti	cho-shotti
৬৫	পঁয়ষট্টি	po-|E|-sho-|T|-ti	poy-shotti
৬৬	ছেষট্টি	che-sho-|T|-ti	cheh-shotti
৬৭	সাতষট্টি	sha-|TH|-sho-|T|-ti	shat-shotti
৬৮	আটষট্টি	ah-|T|-sho-|T|-ti	at-shotti
৬৯	ঊনসত্তর [8]	oh-no-sho-|TH|-tho-|R|	ono-shottoyr

৭০	সত্তর	sho-|TH|-tho-|R|	shottoyr
৭১	একাত্তর	eh-kah-|TH|-tho-|R|	ekattoyr

৭২	বাহাত্তর	ba-ha-|TH|-tho-|R|	*bahattoyr*
৭৩	তিয়াত্তর	thi-ah-|TH|-tho-|R|	*thi-attoyr*
৭৪	চুয়াত্তর	cho-ah-|TH|-tho-|R|	*cho-attoyr*
৭৫	পঁচাত্তর	po-cha-|TH|-tho-|R|	*po-chattoyr*
৭৬	ছিয়াত্তর	chi-ah-|TH|-tho-|R|	*chi-attoyr*
৭৭	সাতাত্তর	cha-tha-|TH|-tho-|R|	*sha-thattoyr*
৭৮	আটাত্তর	ah-ta-|TH|-tho-|R|	*ah-tattoyr*
৭৯	ঊনআশি	oh-no-ah-shi	*ono-ashi*

৮০	আশি	ah-shi	*ashi*
৮১	একাশি	eh-kah-shi	*ekah-shi*
৮২	বিরাশি	bi-ra-shi	*bi-rashi*
৮৩	তিরাশি	thi-ra-shi	*thi-rashi*
৮৪	চুরাশি	cho-ra-shi	*cho-rashi*
৮৫	পঁচাশি	po-cha-shi	*pocha-shi*
৮৬	ছিয়াশি	chi-ah-shi	*chi-ashi*
৮৭	সাতাশি	sha-tha-shi	*sha-thashi*
৮৮	আটাশি	ah-ta-shi	*ata-shi*
৮৯	ঊননব্বই	Oh-no-no-|B|-bo-|E|	*ono-nobboy*

৯০	নব্বই	no-|B|-bo-|E|	*nobboy*
৯১	একানব্বই	eh-kah-no-|B|-bo-|E|	*eka-nobboy*
৯২	বিরানব্বই	bi-rah-no-|B|-bo-|E|	*bira-nobboy*
৯৩	তিরানব্বই	thi-rah-no-|B|-bo-|E|	*thira-nobboy*
৯৪	চুরানব্বই	cho-ra-no-|B|-bo-|E|	*chora-nobboy*
৯৫	পঁচানব্বই	po-cha-no-|B|-bo-|E|	*pocha-nobboy*
৯৬	ছিয়ানব্বই	chi-ah-no-|B|-bo-|E|	*chi-ah-nobboy*
৯৭	সাতানব্বই	sha-tha-no-|B|-bo-|E|	*shatha-nobboy*
৯৮	আটানব্বই	ah-ta-no-|B|-bo-|E|	*ata-nobboy*
৯৯	নিরানব্বই	ni-ra-no-|B|-bo-|E|	*nira-nobboy*

১০০	একশ [10]	eh-|K|-sho	*eksho*
১০০০	এক হাজার	eh-|K| ha-ja-|R|	*ek-hajar*
১০০,০০০	এক লাখ	eh-|K| la-|Kh|	*ek-lakh*
১,০০০,০০০	এক কোটি	eh-|K| koo-ti	*ek-kooti*

1. Individual letters sometimes combine to form a shorthand version. Thus…

Bangla word	চৌদ্দ
Bangla letters	চৌ দ্ দ
Phoneme	cho + |DH| + dho

Thus দ্ + দ combine to form দ্দ

2. Individual letters sometimes combine to form a shorthand version. These shorthand versions can very easily trip the whisky reader however if you break these shorthands to individual units, all makes sense. Thus…

Bangla word	ঊনত্রিশ
Bangla letters	ঊ ন ত্ রি শ
Phoneme	ooh + no + thi + ri + |SH|

Thus ত্ + রি combine to form ত্রি

3. Individual letters sometimes combine to form a shorthand version. Thus…

Bangla word	ঊনচল্লিশ
Bangla letters	ঊ ন চ ল্ লি শ
Phoneme	ooh + no + cho + |L| + Li + |SH|

Thus ল্ + লি combine to form ল্লি

4. Individual letters sometimes combine to form a shorthand version. Thus…

Bangla word	ঊনপঞ্চাশ
Bangla letters	ঊ ন প ঞ্ চা শ
Phoneme	ooh + no + po + |N| + sha + |SH|

Thus ঞ্ + চা combine to form ঞ্চা

5. Individual letters sometimes combine to form a shorthand version. Thus…

Bangla word	একান্ন
Bangla letters	এ কা ন্ ন
Phoneme	eh-ka-|N|-no

Thus ন্ + ন combine to form ন্ন

6. Individual letters sometimes combine to form a shorthand version. Thus…

Bangla word	তিপ্পান্ন
Bangla letters	তি প্ পা ন্ ন
Phoneme	thi-|P|-pa-|N|-no

Thus প্ + পা combine to form প্পা

7 Individual letters sometimes combine to form a shorthand version. Thus…

Bangla word	একষট্টি
Bangla letters	এ ক ষ ট্ টি
Phoneme	eh-|K|-sho-|T|-ti

Thus ট্ + টি combine to form ট্টি

8 Individual letters sometimes combine to form a shorthand version. Thus…

Bangla word	ঊনসত্তর
Bangla letters	ঊ ন স ত্ ত র
Phoneme	oh-no-sho-|TH|-tho-|R|

Thus ত্ + ত combine to form ত্ত

9 Some Bengali letters like ব can combine without forming a shorthand version. Thus…

Bangla word	ঊননব্বই
Bangla letters	ঊ ন ন ব্ ব ই
Phoneme	Oh-no-no-|B|-bo-|E|

Thus ব্ + ব combine to form ব্ব

10 একশ is synonymous with the word কুড়ি

Example 11.0

Large numbers
বড় সংখ্যা
[boro shong-har]

Once the Bengali numbers, one to one hundred is understood and memorized, it is then necessary to understand what happens to larger numbers and their layout. As we use larger numbers with more zero's, the numbers simply add to the chain just as they do with the Roman numerals.

101
One hundred and one

Bangla No.	Bangla word	Phoneme	Transliteration
১০১	একশ এক	eh-|K|-sho eh-|k|	eksho ek

102
One hundred and two

Bangla No.	Bangla word	Phoneme	Transliteration
১০২	একশ দুই	eh-|K|-sho dho-|E|	eksho doi

130
One hundred and thirty

Bangla No.	Bangla word	Phoneme	Transliteration
১৩০	একশ ত্রিশ	eh-|K|-sho tri-|SH|	eksho trish

199
One hundred and ninety-nine

Bangla No.	Bangla word	Phoneme	Transliteration
১৯৯	একশ নিরানব্বই	eh-|K|-sho ni-ra-no-|B|-bo-|E|	eksho nira-nobboy

1,100
One thousand, one hundred

Bangla No.	Bangla word	Phoneme	Transliteration
১,১০০	এক হাজার একশ	eh-|K| ha-ja-|R| eh-|K|-sho	ek-hajar eksho

1,130
One thousand, one hundred and thirty

Bangla No.	Bangla word	Phoneme	Transliteration
১,১৩০	এক হাজার একশ ত্রিশ	eh-|K| ha-ja-|R| eh-|K|-sho tri-|SH|	ek-hajar eksho trish

10,000
Ten thousand

Bangla No.	Bangla word	Phoneme	Transliteration
১০,০০০	দশ হাজার	dho-|SH| ha-ja-|R|	dhosh-hajar

70,000
Seventy thousand

Bangla No.	Bangla word	Phoneme	Transliteration
৭০,০০০	সত্তর হাজার	sho-|TH|-tho-|R| ha-ja-|R|	shottoyr-hajar

110,000
One hundred thousand and ten thousand

Bangla No.	Bangla word	Phoneme	Transliteration
১১০,০০০	এক লাখ দশ হাজার	eh-|K| la-|Kh| dho-|SH| ha-ja-|R|	ek-lakh dhosh-hajar

1,900,000
One million and nine hundred thousand

Bangla No.	Bangla word	Phoneme	Transliteration
১,৯০০,০০০	এক কোটি নয় লাখ	eh-|K| koo-ti no-|E| la-|Kh|	ek-kooti noy-lakh

Example 11.1

Conversation
আলাপ
[ah-lap]

এই বইয়ের দাম কি? *
This, book's price, what?
(What is this book's price?)

এই বইয়ের দাম একুশ টাকা ।
This, book's price, 21 taka.
(This book's price is 21 taka.)

ওটা বাড়ির দাম কত? *
That, houses price, how many?
(How much is that house?)

বাড়ির দাম দুই লাখ ত্রিশ হাজার দুইশ দশ টাকা ।
Houses price, two hundred thousand, thirty thousand, two hundred, ten takas.
(The house's price is two hundred and thirty thousand, two hundred and 10 takas.)
(The car's price is 230,210 taka.)

কারিমা আপনার বয়স কত?
Karima, your, age, how many?
(Karima, what is your age?)

আমি বারো বছর বয়সী ।
I, twelve, year, old.
(I am twelve years old)

সাবিরা আপনার বয়স কত?
Sabira, your, age, how many?
(Sabira, what is your age?)

আমার বয়স এগারো।
My, age, eleven.
(My age is eleven.)

তামান্না আপনি কি কাজ করো?
Tamanna, you, what, work, do?
(Tamanna, what work do you do?)

আমি সলিসিটার।
I, Solicitor.
(I am a solicitor.)

আপনার বেতন কি?
Your, salary, what?
(What is your salary?)

আমার বেতন বিয়াল্লিশ হাজার টাকা।
My, salary, forty-two thousand takas.
(My salary is forty-two thousand taka.)
(My salary is 42,000 taka.)

কৈঢা বাজে?
What is the time?
(What is the time?)

একটা বাজো।
One o'clock is.
(It is one o'clock.)

ভাই এখন কটা বাজে?
Brother, now, what is the time?
(Brother, what is the time now?)

এখন একটা চল্লিশ বাজে। |
Now, one forty [1:40] is.
(It is one forty [1:40] now.)

এই বইয়ের দাম কি? *
This, book's price, what?
(What is this book's price?)

বইয়ের দাম পাঁচ টাকা। |
Book's price, five takas.
(The book's price is five taka.)

*note you can say either "what?" or "how much?" Both work.

New words
নতুন শব্দ

Bangla word	Translation	Transliteration
দাম	Price	*daam*
বয়স	Age	*bo-esh*
বছর	Year	*bo-chor*
কাজ	Work [Employment]	*kaj*
করো	Do (it)	*koroh*
সলিসিটার	Solicitor	*solicitor*
বেতন	Salary	*beh-ton*

Lesson 12.0 – Forming words. Plural Nouns

We have introduced various nouns so far. Such nouns are inherently in the singular form. Let us now introduce what this looks like in the plural form and how it can be utlised in sentences.

In the English language, the plural form of most nouns is achieved by adding the letter "S" to the end of the noun.

Cat. Cats.
Chair. Chairs.
Car. Cars.

There are of course exceptions. Words ending with the phoneme "ch" and "s" usually add "es" to the singular noun to become plural.

Bus. Buses.
Church. Churches.
Box. Boxes.

Words ending with the phoneme "fe" and "f" usually add "ves" to the singular noun to become plural.

Leaf. Leaves.
Wolf. Wolves.
Life. Lives.

There are various other exceptions. The previous examples being most common.

Fortunately, the plural form in the Bengali script is much more straightforward. Let us now look at some of these.

Bangla Example No. 1 –

Bangla noun	গাড়ি

Possessive form of Bangla noun	গাড়িগুলো
Example sentence	আমার গাড়িগুলো ।
Transliteration	amar garee-gooloo
Translation	My cars.

Bangla Example No. 2 –

Bangla noun	বই

Possessive form of Bangla noun	বইগুলো
Example sentence	আমার বইগুলো ।
Transliteration	amar boi-gooloo
Translation	My books.

Bangla Example No. 3 –

Bangla noun	গাছ

Possessive form of Bangla noun	গাছগুলো
Example sentence	গাছগুলো সাদা ।
Transliteration	gach-gooloo shada
Translation	Trees are white

Bangla Example No. 4 –

Bangla noun	ফুল

Possessive form of Bangla noun	ফুলগুলো
Example sentence	ফুলগুলো সুন্দর হয় ।
Transliteration	fool-gooloo shondor hoy
Translation	Flowers are beautiful

Bangla Example No. 5 –

Bangla noun	গরু

Possessive form of Bangla noun	গরুগুলো
Example sentence	গরুগুলো সেখানে আছে ।
Transliteration	goroo-gooloo she-kaneh ache
Translation	Cows are there

Thus the plural form of singular nouns are formed by adding "গুলো" to the end of the noun in question.

Note, however, when the noun is preceded with a number, the plural form is no longer required.

Thus when a number is indicated, "গুলো" no longer needs to be utilised.

Example 12.0

Conversation
আলাপ
[ah-lap]

আবদুল এখানে কত আম আছে?
Abdul, here, how many mangoes, is?
(Abdul, how many mangoes are here?)

এখানে দশটা আম আছে |
Here, ten mangoes, there is.
(There are ten mangoes here.)

আবদুল এখানে কত আম আছে?
Abdul, here, how many mangoes, is?
(Abdul, how many mangoes are here?)

এখানে অনেক আম গুলো আছে|
Here, many mangoes, is.
(There are many mangoes here.)

সেখানে থেকে আম গুলো আনো |
There, from, mangoes, bring it.
(From there, bring the mangoes.)

সেখানে থেকে দুটা আম আনো |
There, from, two mangoes, bring it.
(From there, bring two mangoes.)

New words
নতুন শব্দ

Bangla word	Translation	Transliteration
গরু	Cow	*go-roo*

All new words

A

Age	বয়স
All / Everything	সব
And / Moreover	এবং

B

Ball	বল
Balagonj	বালাগঞ্জ
Balloon	বেলুন
Bangladesh	বাংলাদেশ
Banana	কলা
Beautiful	সুন্দর
Big	বড়
Bird	পাখি
Birthday	জন্মদিন
Black	কালো
Black pepper	গোলমরিচ
Blue	নীল
Brick	ইট
Brother / Brothers	ভাই
Brown	বাদামী
Boat	নৌকা
Book	বই

C

Car	গাড়ি
Capital (city)	রাজধানী
Chair	চেয়ার
Cheap	সস্তা
Coat	কোট
Cold	ঠান্ডা
Colour	রঙ
Continents	মহাদেশ
Country	দেশ
Cow	গরু
Curd	দই

D

Dad (Daddy)	বাবা
Daughter	মেয়ে
Difficult	কঠিন
Do (it)	করো
Dog	কুকুর
Doll	পুতুল
Door	দরজা

E

Eight	আট
Elephant	হাতি
Expensive	দামী

F

Fast	দুত
Five	পাঁচ
Flower	ফুল
Four	চার
From	থেকে
Full	পুরো

G

Green	সবুজ
Grey	ধূসর
Gold	সোনা

H

Happy	শুভ
Happy Birthday!	শুভ জন্মদিন
He / She / It	সে
here	এখানে
Him / Her	তাকে
His / Her	তার
Home/House	বাসা
Horse	ঘোড়া
House / Home	বাড়ি
Hot	গরম
How many?	কত / কতগুলো
How much?	কৈঢা

I

I	আমি
is	হয়
Is doing	করছে

J

Juice of a fruit/sap	রস

K

Key	চাবি

L

Leaf	পাতা
Love	ভালোবাসি

M

Mango	আম
Me	আমাকে
Milk	দুধ
Mosque	মসজিদ
My	আমার

N

Name	নাম
New	নতুন
Nine	নয়
No	না
Now	এখন

O

OK	ঠিক আছে
Old	পুরাতন
One	এক
Orange	কমলা

P

Pen	কলম
Pink	গোলাপী
Price	দাম
Purple	বেগুনি

R

Reading	পড়ছে
Red	লাল
Right	ঠিক
River	নদী

S

Salary	বেতন
Salt	লবণ
Seven	সাত
Six	ছয়
Sister / Sisters	বোন
Slow	ধীরে
Small	ছোট
Solicitor	সলিসিটার
Son	ছেলে

Strong	শক্তিশালী
Student / Students	ছাত্র
Sugar	চিনি
Surname	ডাকনাম
Sweet	মিঠা
Sylhet	সিলেট

T

Table	টেবিল
Taka / Money	টাকা
Tea	চা
Ten	দশ
Their	তাদের
There is/That is	আছে
They	তারা
This	এটা
That	ওটা
Thank you	ধন্যবাদ
There	সেখানে
Three	তিন
Those	সেগুলো
Today	আজ
Tomato	টমেটো
Tomorrow	আগামীকাল
Tree	গাছ
Two	দুই

U

Us / Our	আমাদের
Uncle	চাচা

V

Very	খুব
Village	গ্রাম

W

Water	পানি
Watch	ঘড়ি
We	আমরা
We are also	আমরাও
Weak	দুর্বল
What?	কি?
When?	কবে
Where?	কোথায়
Which?	কোন
White	সাদা
Who?	কে?
Work [Employment]	কাজ

Y

Year	বছর
Yellow	হলুদ
Yes	হাঁ
You	তুমি / আপনি / তোমাকে
Your	তোমার / আপনার

Additional words

Nouns / Adjective / Verb

English	Bengali
Breakfast	নাস্তা
Button	বোতাম
Candle	মোমবাতি
Dine	খানা
Delicious / fun	মজা
Happy	খুশি [1]
Profit	লাভ
Sleeping	ঘুমান
Market	বাজার
Socks	মোজা
Wax	মোম

[1] also known as শুভ

Fruits

English	Bengali
Apple	আপেল
Lemon	লেবু
Pear	নাশপাতি
Pineapple	আনারস
Watermelon	তরমুজ

Animals

English	Bengali
Bear	ভালুক
Deer	হরিণ
Donkey	গাধা
Fish	মাছ
Sheep	ভেড়ী
Tiger	বাঘ
Whale	তিমি

Family members

English	Bengali
Aunt (paternal)	ফুফু
Aunt (maternal)	খালা
Uncle (paternal)	চাচা [2]
Uncle (maternal)	মামা [3]
Grandfather (paternal)	দাদা [4]
Grandmother (maternal)	দাদী [5]
Grandfather (maternal)	নানা
Grandmother (maternal)	নানী

[2 3] also known as কাকা

[4] also known as দাদু

[5] also known as দিদা

Body parts

English	Bengali
Belly	পেট
Eyes	চোখ
Fingers	আঙ্গুল
Hands	হাত
Head	মাথা
Mouth	মুখ
Lips	ঠোঁট

Bibliography

Dr Anwar Dil and Dr Afia Dil 2011, Bengali Language Movement and Creation of Bangladesh, 2nd edn, Adorn Books & Intercultural Forum, Dhaka.

Srinath Raghavan 2013, 1971 A Global History of the Creation of Bangladesh, 1st edn, Havard University Press, London.

Willem Van Schendel 2009, A History of Bangladesh, 1st edn, Cambridge University Press, Cambridge.

Bijay Chandra Mazumdar 2007, The History of the Bengali Language, 4th edn, Hardpress Publishing, Miami.

Printed in Great Britain
by Amazon